PLAYING WITH
MAGNETS

Created and produced by
NW Books, 28 Percy Street
London W1P OLD

First published in the United States in 1995 by
Copper Beech Books, an imprint of
The Millbrook Press, 2 Old New Milford Road
Brookfield, Connecticut 06804

Editor:
Susannah Le Besque

Design:
David West Children's Book Design
Illustrator:
Tony Kenyon
Photography:
Roger Vlitos
Consultant:
Dr. Bryson Gore

*The publishers wish to point out
that all the photographs reproduced
in this book have been posed by models.*

Library of Congress Cataloging-in-Publication Data
Gibson, Gary, 1957-
Playing with magnets / by Gary Gibson : illustrated by
Tony Kenyon. p. cm. -- (Science for fun)
Includes index.
ISBN 1-56294-615-3 (lib. bdg.)
ISBN 1-56294-633-1 (pbk.)
1. Magnets--Juvenile literature. 2.
Magnets--Experiments--Juvenile literature.
[1. Magnets--Experiments. 2. Experiments.] I.
Kenyon, Tony, ill. II. Title. III. Series: Gibson,
Gary. 1957- Science for fun
QC757.5.G53   1995   94-41188
538'.078--dc20   CIP AC

SCIENCE FOR FUN

PLAYING WITH MAGNETS

GARY GIBSON

COPPER BEECH BOOKS
Brookfield, Connecticut

CONTENTS

WHAT IS A MAGNET? **6**

LONG-RANGE FORCE **8**

THROUGH AND THROUGH **10**

CHAIN REACTION **12**

MAGNETIC METALS **14**

PUSH AND PULL **16**

USEFUL MAGNETS **18**

VERY ATTRACTIVE **20**

INVISIBLE PATTERNS **22**

NORTH AND SOUTH **24**

HIDDEN MAGNETS **26**

ELECTROMAGNETISM **28**

FANTASTIC MAGNET FACTS **30**

GLOSSARY **31**

INDEX **32**

INTRODUCTION

Have you ever wondered where magnetism comes from? Did you know that there are two types of magnets?

Magnets have many uses. They are used to keep refrigerator doors shut and to enable ships and aircraft to find their way around the world.

Scientists have found out many things about magnets and magnetism. This book contains a selection of exciting "hands-on" projects to help explain some of these fascinating discoveries.

GET AN ADULT TO HELP YOU WITH THIS

Whenever this symbol appears adult supervision is required.

WHAT IS A MAGNET?

People have known about magnets for thousands of years. The first magnets were made out of black rocks called lodestones which are found naturally in the ground. Some metal objects are attracted to this rock. Modern magnets are made from steel. They can be made into almost any shape – horseshoe, bar or ring.

MAKE A FISHING GAME

1 Draw some fish shapes on thin cardboard. Color them in and cut them out. Attach a steel paper clip to each fish.

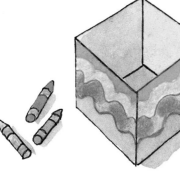

2 Find a large, clean cardboard box. Decorate the outside so that it looks like the water in a pond.

3 Make two fishing rods. Tie a 30-inch long piece of string to each stick. Tape a magnet to the end of the string.

4 Using the fishing rods, compete with a friend to see who can "catch" the most fish.

WHY IT WORKS

Magnet

Force

Magnets "attract" some metals, meaning they pull some metals toward them. This pull is called magnetic force. You can feel this force when you pull the paper clip off the magnet.

We call objects that are attracted to magnets, magnetic.

FURTHER IDEAS

Collect together any objects you think may be magnetic. Try objects such as nails, screws, knitting needles, pins and aluminum foil. Make a list of the objects that are attracted to your magnet.

LONG-RANGE FORCE

How far away can the magnetic force work? Scientists use magnets that will attract objects from many feet away. Your magnet can attract objects a few inches away. When a magnet and object touch, they "stick" together as if fixed with glue.

GET AN ADULT TO HELP YOU WITH THIS

MAKE A FLYING BUTTERFLY

1 Find a clean cardboard box. Ask an adult to cut away two opposite sides leaving a "U" shape (shown right).

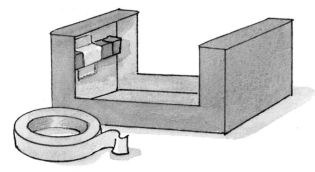

2 Tape a strong bar-shaped magnet along one side of the box (see left).

3 On thin paper, draw and cut out a butterfly shape. Push a thumbtack into one wing (see right). Tie a length of thread to the tack.

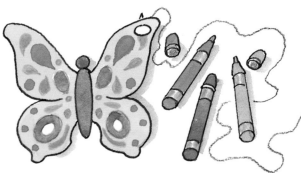

4 Tape the loose end of the thread to the side of the box opposite the magnet. When the thread is pulled taut, the butterfly should almost touch the magnet.

5 Stand the box up so the magnet is at the top. Hold the butterfly just below the magnet and let it float. Adjust the length of the thread to get the best floating effect.

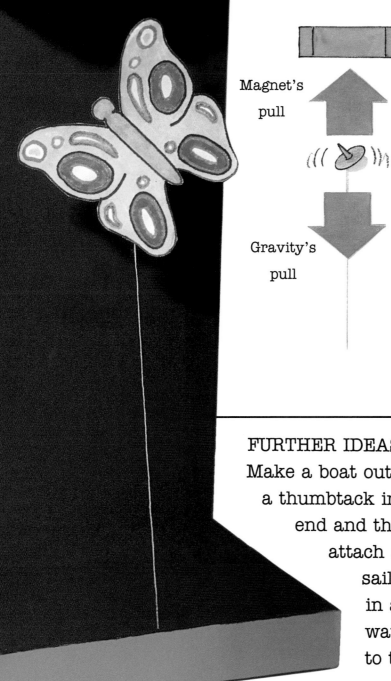

Magnet's pull

Gravity's pull

WHY IT WORKS

The magnet is strong enough to attract the thumbtack from about an inch away. The magnetic pull on the thumbtack is strong enough to overcome the force of gravity trying to pull the tack to the ground. This leaves the butterfly floating in mid-air.

FURTHER IDEAS

Make a boat out of cork. Push a thumbtack into one end and then attach a paper sail. Float it in a bowl of water. Now hold a magnet close to the boat and see if it moves.

THROUGH AND THROUGH

You can stick paper notes to the metal door of a refrigerator with a magnet. The paper and paint cannot block the magnetic force. If the magnetism is strong enough it can work straight through materials as if they were not there. This can be useful for making things move without touching them.

MAKE A RACING GAME

1 Draw and color in a race track on a large sheet of thick cardboard. Mark the starting/finishing line clearly.

2 Draw two racing cars on thin cardboard. Cut them out and color them. Tape a small magnet to the underside of each.

3  Find four cardboard tubes of the same size. Place one under each corner of the race track so it is raised.

4 Find two long, thin sticks. Tape a small magnet to one end of each.

5 You can move your car with the magnet from underneath the race track. Race against a friend, taking care not to mix up each other's cars!

WHY IT WORKS

The magnets under the car and on the stick are attracted to each other. The magnetic force goes through the race track, although the race track does slightly weaken the force.

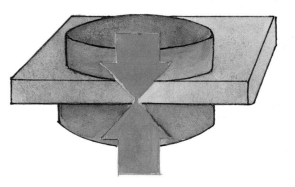

FURTHER IDEAS
Without getting your fingers wet, try to remove a steel paper clip from a glass of water. Move your magnet along the outside of the glass.

CHAIN REACTION

You may have noticed that when magnetic metals touch a magnet they will attract magnetic metals too. We can use this characteristic to build a "chain" of magnetic objects outward from a permanent magnet. Permanent magnets stay magnetic unless they are dropped or get too hot.

MAKE A MAGNETIC SCULPTURE

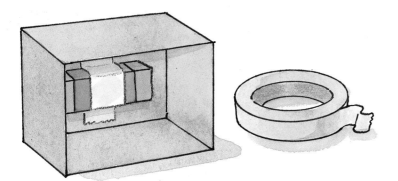

1 Find a small cardboard box. Tape a small magnet to the inside of the bottom of the box. Turn the box upside down.

2 Decorate the box with your own pattern and color it with bright colors.

3 Place a few steel paper clips on top of the box above the magnet. Build up a sculpture by adding pins, tacks and nails.

4 Change the shape until you are satisfied with your sculpture. You can reshape it endlessly.

WHY IT WORKS

When a magnetic metal is attracted to a permanent magnet it becomes a magnet too. It can attract other objects but only while it is touching a permanent magnet. This is called "induced" magnetism.

FURTHER IDEAS
Hang a magnet over the edge of a box and tape it into place. Try to form a chain by hanging paper clips from the end of the magnet.

MAGNETIC METALS

There are many different metals, but only three pure metals can be magnetized. These are iron, nickel and cobalt. None of the other pure metals – gold, silver, aluminum – can be made into magnets. But if you mix pure metals together their magnetic characteristics can be altered.

MAKE A COIN TESTER

GET AN ADULT TO HELP YOU WITH THIS

1 Ask an adult to cut a slot at one end of a shoe box (see right). The slot should be just bigger than your largest coin.

2 Cut out a strip of cardboard. Fold into an "L" shape. Tape into place just to the left of the slot.

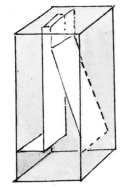

3 Cut another strip of cardboard, creasing it 3/4 of an inch from the top. Tape this end to the right of the slot. Tape the other end to the side of the box.

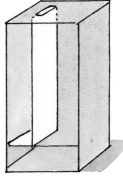

4 Cut another strip of cardboard. Fold into the shape shown (right). Make sure it fits into the triangular space between the first pieces.

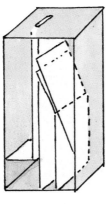

5 Find a strong magnet. Tape it inside the box just to the right of the slot.

6 Drop your coins into the slot. Most will fall to the left side of the box. If you drop iron or steel washers into the slot they will fall to the right side of the box.

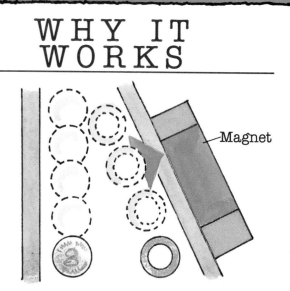

Magnet

Most coins are made from non-magnetic metals such as a copper mix. When you drop them into the box they are not attracted to the magnet and so fall straight down. When you drop iron or steel objects they are attracted by the magnet and are pulled over to the right side of the box.

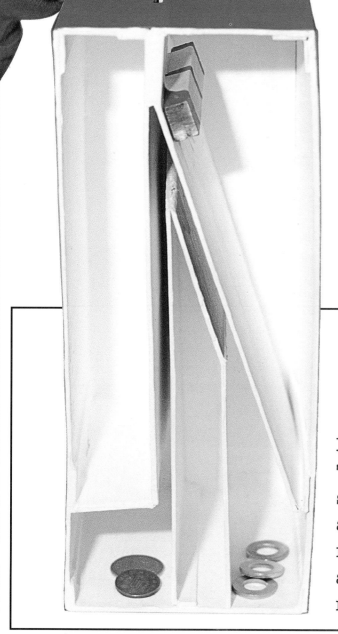

FURTHER IDEAS
Tableware is often made of stainless steel. Make a ramp out of cardboard and roll spoons or forks down it. Put a magnet under the ramp. See how it affects the path of the tableware. Why not try toy cars as well.

PUSH AND PULL

Magnets have two points where their power is strongest. These are called poles. Every magnet has a north and a south pole. When iron or steel touches a permanent magnet it has poles too (see pages 12-13). A good way of testing whether an object is a permanent magnet or not is to see if it will "repel" or push away another magnet.

MAKE A MAGNET FLOAT

1 Find a cardboard box. Ask an adult to cut away the sides and the middle of the box to leave the shape (shown at right).

GET AN ADULT TO HELP YOU WITH THIS

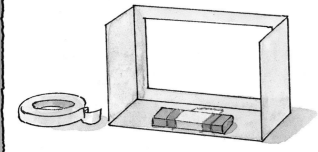

2 Tape down a strong bar magnet to the base of the box (left).

3 Copy the shape (shown at right) onto a piece of cardboard and cut out. Tape an identical magnet to the cardboard. Fold the cardboard around the magnet.

N   S

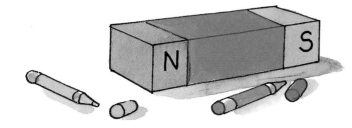

N   S

4 Hold the second magnet on top of the first with both north and south poles facing the same way. Tape together.

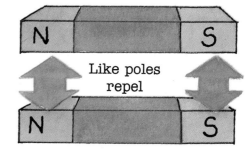

N   S

Like poles repel

N   S

5 The top magnet should "float" above the bottom. Try pushing the top magnet.

Magnetic poles of the same type repel each other. Gravity is trying to pull the top magnet down, but the two magnets are repelling each other with such force that the top one is held above the bottom. The top magnet would spring away if it wasn't taped in place.

FURTHER IDEAS

Find three horseshoe-shaped magnets. Thread them onto two pencils (shown at right). Line up the poles. See if you can make the magnets float. Try doing the same thing with ring-shaped magnets. Which works best?

USEFUL MAGNETS

Doctors have used magnets to pull tiny bits of iron out of a patient's eye. The advantage of using a magnet is that nothing needs to touch the injured eye. The magnet's ability to attract some materials but not others has been used in many ways. Giant magnets are used to sort out different waste metals.

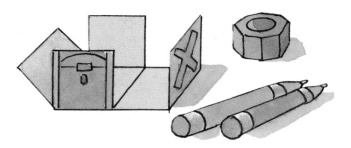

MAKE A TREASURE HUNT

 1 Make a desert island by filling a bowl almost to the top with clean, dry sand.

2 Make a palm tree using part of a large plastic drinking straw as the stem. Attach some green paper leaves to it with tape. Plant it on your island.

 3 Make a treasure chest out of colored cardboard. Now find some treasure to put in it. An iron or steel bolt will do.

4 Bury the treasure chest in the sand. Make sure it is fairly near to the surface.

5 Search for the treasure using a magnet. You can take turns with a friend to find it.

WHY IT WORKS

Magnet

Treasure

You can hunt for the treasure by moving the magnet over the surface of the sand. When you hold the magnet directly over the steel treasure, the magnet strongly attracts it. The magnetic force goes straight through the sand.

FURTHER IDEAS
Sort out aluminum soda cans that can be recycled by testing each can with a magnet. Aluminum cans are not magnetic.

VERY ATTRACTIVE

Magnets pull magnetic materials such as iron and steel toward them. This pull is called attraction. The stronger the magnet, the stronger its attractive force. Modern household items have many ingenious uses for magnetic attraction. Did you know that a magnet is often used on a refrigerator door to hold it firmly closed?

MAKE A FUNNY FACE

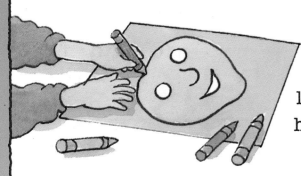

1 Draw the shape of a face on a sheet of thin cardboard. Make the eyes, nose and mouth especially large. Don't draw in any hair or eyebrows.

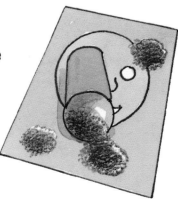

2 Ask an adult to make some iron filings for you by filing down a nail. Pour the iron filings onto the cardboard in a few places.

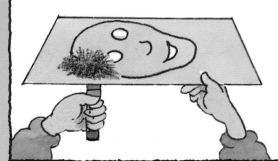

3 Hold the cardboard with one hand and bring a magnet under it with the other. The magnet will attract the iron filings through the cardboard.

4 Arrange the iron filings with the magnet to give your face hair, eyebrows and a beard. Move the magnet away from your funny face.

WHY IT WORKS

Magnetic force

Magnet

The magnetic force pulls on each tiny piece of iron filing. As you move the magnet under the cardboard the filings are dragged along. When you move the magnet away the iron filings stay in place.

FURTHER IDEAS

Test the strength of your magnet. Use it to move a pin through one page of a book, then through two pages, then three pages and so on until the pages block the magnetic force.

INVISIBLE PATTERNS

Magnetic objects close to a magnet are attracted to it. There is a "field" (space) around the magnet where the magnetic force works. We cannot see this field but can feel its pull on objects. Scientists have discovered that birds use the Earth's magnetic field to guide them on long journeys.

SEE A MAGNETIC FIELD

1 Use a pair of compasses to draw a circle on a sheet of cardboard. Cut out the circle and tape a bar magnet in the center.

2 Turn the cardboard over so the magnet is underneath. Evenly sprinkle some iron filings (see page 20) over the surface of the cardboard.

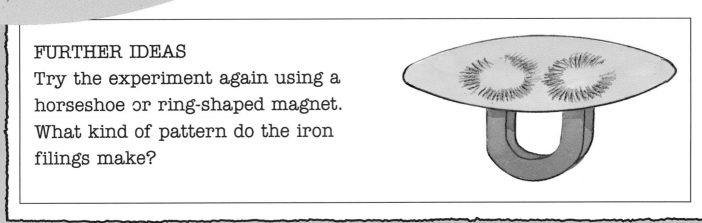

3 Gently tap the cardboard. Examine the pattern made by the filings. You will see that the filings form lines. These show you where the magnetic field lies.

WHY IT WORKS

Lines of force

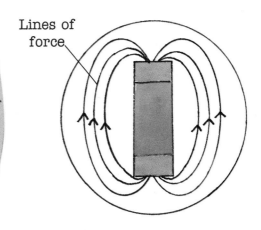

Each filing is attracted to the magnet along invisible lines of force. These make up the magnetic field. The filings are small enough to show the direction in which the field is pulling.

FURTHER IDEAS

Try the experiment again using a horseshoe or ring-shaped magnet. What kind of pattern do the iron filings make?

NORTH AND SOUTH

For centuries travelers have found their way with the help of a compass. Inside a compass is a small magnetic pointer. It spins around but always comes to rest pointing north. From knowing where north is, it is easy to locate south, west and east.

MAKE A COMPASS

1 Stroke a nail with one end of a magnet. Make sure you pass the magnet in one direction only. Stroke the nail about 20 times.

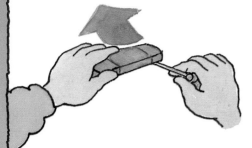

2 Ask an adult to slice a piece of cork. Now tape the magnetized nail to it.

GET AN ADULT TO HELP YOU WITH THIS

3 Float the cork in a basin of water. Leave until the nail stops moving. Make sure there are no magnetic objects nearby.

WHY IT WORKS

4 The nail will point either north or south. Find out which way it is pointing, then make labels for north, south, west and east.

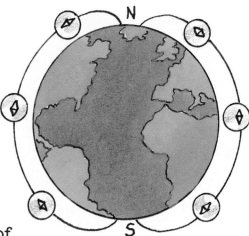

The north pole of a magnet seeks out the north pole of the Earth. It is as if the Earth contained a gigantic magnet. The north pole of the Earth attracts any smaller magnets so that when allowed to, they always point north.

FURTHER IDEAS
Tie a piece of thread around the middle of a bar magnet. Suspend the magnet from the back of a chair. Watch to see if the poles point north-south. What happens when other magnetic objects are close to the magnet?

HIDDEN MAGNETS

You may be surprised how important magnets are in modern machines. Computers use magnetic floppy disks to store huge amounts of information. Tape recorders and video recorders use magnetic tape to store film, sound and music. These are hidden magnets.

THE AMAZING MAGIC FINGER

 Magnetize a steel nail by stroking it in one direction with a magnet. Stroke at least 20 times (see page 24).

2 Carefully tape the nail to your index finger. Make sure the point cannot hurt anyone.

 Find an old glove that fits your hand snugly. Put it on to hide the magnetized nail.

4 Bring your magic finger close to a compass needle. Amaze your friends by making the compass needle swing around.

Unmagnetized nail   Magnetized nail

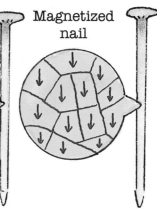

The metal in the nail is made up of millions of tiny crystals. Each can behave like a tiny magnet but they point in different directions.

Stroking the nail with a magnet makes each crystal point the same way. This causes the nail to become magnetized.

FURTHER IDEAS
Use your magic finger for other magic tricks. Impress your friends by balancing a pin or nail right on the end of your finger.

ELECTROMAGNETISM

An electromagnet is a coil of wire around an iron core. You may have seen a crane that has an electromagnet instead of a hook to carry things. Powerful electromagnets can lift heavy iron loads, even whole cars. The load is dropped by switching off the electromagnet.

MAKE AN ELECTROMAGNET

1 Take a cardboard box. Make holes in the center of three sides. Cut two strips of cardboard. Make three holes in each strip (see right).

Holes

2 Push three pieces of stick through the holes in the strips of cardboard and the box (left). This is your crane arm.

3 Color some smaller boxes to make them look like cars or an iron bar. Glue a steel washer to the top of each one.

4 Take two to three feet of plastic-coated wire and coil around an iron nail. Connect the wire to the terminals of a battery.

5 Hide the battery in the box. Push the nail and wire through the hole in the front of the crane. Use the electromagnet to pick up paper clips. Switch it off by removing the wire from the battery.

WHY IT WORKS

Nail becomes magnetized

Electricity flowing along a wire has a magnetic field around it. The field is made stronger by coiling the wire. The nail inside the coils becomes magnetized by the field. Each part of the iron nail lines up facing the same direction, running from north to south.

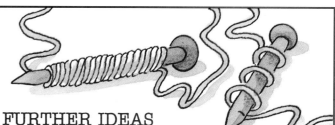

FURTHER IDEAS
Experiment with your electromagnet by changing the number of coils around the nail. What happens when there are fewer coils? What happens when there are more?

FANTASTIC MAGNET FACTS

Until the 13th century people believed that magnets were magical. Then a Frenchman, Petrus de Maricourt, discovered (in 1269) that magnets have two poles and the mysteries of magnetism started to be unraveled. In 1600, an English physician named William Gilbert discovered the Earth's magnetism.

Why does the Earth behave like a giant magnet with a magnetic field surrounding it? Scientists have found out that the magnetic field is produced by the molten metal which is found deep beneath the Earth's surface. As the Earth spins, electric currents are created in the molten metal and these currents produce the Earth's magnetic field.

The largest electromagnet is higher than a four-story building and has an enormous aluminum coil weighing 1,100 tons. The magnet was built by a team of Russian and Swiss scientists and is made out of more metal than the Eiffel tower in Paris!

Did you know that some animals have a built-in magnet that acts like a compass and helps them to find their way? Whales and dolphins use the Earth's magnetic field to navigate. Scientists have discovered that if a magnet is fixed to a pigeon's back it cannot find its way on cloudy days.

The world's heaviest magnet is in the Joint Institute for Nuclear Research near Moscow, Russia. It measures 196 feet in diameter and weighs a massive 42,000 tons.

In Australia there are insects called Compass Termites which build their nests facing north. It is thought they use the Earth's magnetism to get the position of their nests right.

The amazingly fast Maglev trains use magnetic force to help them reach speeds of over 217 miles an hour. The Japanese MLU system uses electromagnets that repel each other so the train floats above the rails.

GLOSSARY

Attract
To pull something toward you.

Compass
An instrument with a magnetized pointer. The pointer always points north because it always lines itself with the Earth's magnetic field.

Electromagnet
A coil of wire with an iron bar inside it. It becomes a magnet only when electricity is flowing through the coil.

Force
Anything that can cause a push or a pull.

Induced magnetism
Magnetism caused in magnetic material such as iron or steel, when a permanent magnet is brought very close.

Line of force
A line that shows the magnetic effect around a magnet.

Lodestone
A type of rock which is a natural magnet.

Magnetic field
The space around a magnet where the magnetic force works.

Magnetic material
Material that can be made into or attracted to a magnet.

Magnetic pole
Place on a magnet where the magnetic force is strongest. Poles can be north and south.

Magnetize
To turn a magnetic material into a magnet.

Permanent magnet
A magnet that keeps its magnetism unless it is dropped, knocked or gets too hot.

Repel
To push apart. Two south or two north poles repel each other.

INDEX

aluminum 19
animals and magnetism 22, 30
attraction 7, 8, 9, 20, 31

bar magnets 6, 25
birds 22, 30

chain of magnetic objects 12
coin tester 14-15
compass 24-25, 27, 31
Compass Termites 30
computers 26
cranes 28

Earth's magnetic field 25, 30
electric currents 30
electromagnets 28-29, 30

fishing game 6
floating magnet 16-17
flying butterfly 8-9
funny face 20-21

gravity 9, 17

hidden magnets 26
horseshoe-shaped magnets 6, 17, 23
household uses 20

induced magnetism 13, 31

iron 14, 15, 16
iron filings 20, 21, 22, 23

largest and heaviest magnets 30
line of force 23, 31
lodestones 6, 31

Maglev trains 30
magnetic field 22, 23, 29, 30, 31
magnetic force 7, 8, 10, 11, 21, 22
magnetic materials 7, 14, 20, 31
magnetic poles 16, 17, 30, 31
magnetic sculpture 12-13
magnetizing objects 26-27, 31

navigation 22, 24, 30
non-magnetic metals 15
north pole 25

permanent magnets 12, 13, 16, 31
pure metals 14

racing game 10-11
repulsion 16, 17, 30, 31
ring-shaped magnets 6, 17, 23

steel 6, 15, 16
steel nails 26-27

treasure hunt 18-19